Flirting

Stewart Ferris

summersdale

Summersdale Publishers Ltd
46 West Street
Chichester
PO19 1RP
United Kingdom

www.summersdale.com

ISBN 1 84024 235 3

By the same author:
How to Chat-up Babes
The Little Book of Chat-up Lines

Contents

Introduction	4
A Made-up History of Flirting	7
Talking	12
Physical contact	25
Body language	36
Chat-up lines	50
Flirting on the Internet ,e-mail and texting	62
Premium rate telephone services	64
Dating agencies	66
Alcohol	68
Taking it to the edge	70
How far can you go with a stranger?	73
When does flirting become cheating?	74
The worst that can happen	77
Making someone want to flirt with you	79
Your internal characteristics	81
Your external characteristics	96
Getting rid of a persistent flirt	106
Stalking	111
Flirting in competition	113
On the rebound	116
How do you know if someone is flirting with you?	118
Develop your own flirting style	120
Top 10 do's and don'ts for flirting	122
The personality test	124

Introduction

Flirting is fun, but it's risky. Many people enjoy flirting simply *because* it's so risky. Flirting involves putting your whole outward appearance and inner personality on the line. You're basically asking a stranger if they fancy you, and if they don't, it's going to hurt. If they do fancy you and your husband or wife later finds out, it's going to hurt even more.

That's why the phrase 'flirting with danger' is apt. Flirting is one of the most dangerous aspects of modern society. It's similar to skiing off-piste, only more people have their legs broken at cocktail parties than on mountainsides.★

Anyone can learn to flirt. It's about taking control of an interaction with someone and steering it in a romantic direction. Some people have sufficient natural charisma to cause a spark in others when communicating. For the rest of us there are many easy ways to ignite a flame: a few simple tips and a little self-control

★ This is a lie.

will transform anyone's flirting technique. Failing that, try a box of matches.

If you want to flirt without the risk of getting hurt, make sure you have the correct safety gear: a good understanding of body language; a reasonable-sounding excuse for when you get caught out; and a secure helmet. It might also help to keep this book in your pocket. You'll be glad to have these 128 pages of advice next to your body if things go wrong and someone hits you there.

A made-up history of flirting

Flirting goes back to the dawn of life on earth. In the primeval soup of pre-history the first single-celled male organism would nervously go up to a female cell on a Friday night and clumsily offer to buy her a drink. If it wasn't for those first fumbling attempts at communicating with the opposite sex there would have been no evolution to the point where today complex multicellular male humans nervously go up to females on a Friday night and clumsily offer to buy them a drink.

Men and women throughout history have developed their own ways of flirting. Viking men a thousand years ago flirted with women by killing their husbands, burning their houses and inserting their penises without permission. Later, a misguided King Henry VIII flirted with girls by cutting their heads off. Jane Austen flirted with men by talking to them in convoluted, turgid Georgian prose that sent them into a deep coma, thus enabling her to do whatever she wanted to them.

Victorian times saw the arrival of flirting techniques that almost brought humanity to a sudden halt. Body language was made impossible because everyone was so covered up with layers of unnecessary clothing that no one knew if they had any bodies. Any male/female contact was only possible in the presence of a vicar or a doctor.

The most popular chat-up line of the time was,

'if I verbally articulated the splendour and unblemished beauty of your physicality, would it in any way prejudice your sentiments with regard to the individual who habitually refers to himself by the perpendicular pronoun?'★

With these restrictions, the growth in population slowed considerably.

In recent times, the range of sophisticated and subtle flirting

★ If I said you had a beautiful body would you hold it against me?

techniques has increased. You can offer to buy the other person any one of a number of different kinds of drink, and it doesn't always have to be on a Friday night.

Talking

If you are one of those people fortunate enough not to lose the power of speech when approaching someone, you can try engaging them in some kind of conversation. This is not recommended for beginners, as it opens a minefield of potential complications, problems and mines.

The aim of talking to someone in a flirtatious manner is to ascertain the likelihood of them letting you into their underwear without the need for a general anaesthetic on their part(s). But when we talk flirtatiously we speak in code. This is why people aren't always aware that someone is flirting with them.

The reason for speaking in code is to reduce the embarrassment of rejection. If you come out with a blatant phrase like 'I'd like to see you naked' or 'I hope I can get to shag you without you seeing me naked', your intention is as obvious as the humiliation you will shortly suffer. By avoiding direct mention of your desired romantic liaison, you can test the water gently.

Ambiguity is the key to saving face. When you skirt around the subject of romance by making subtle allusions to sex, you're checking out the other person's barriers. You might find a way in immediately, or you might find that they slowly lower their defences as they grow more comfortable in your presence. But because you're talking carefully in code, the other person has the opportunity at any time to pull the barriers back up by changing the subject. If this happens, the humiliation is minimal. Everything has been kept implicit, no direct sexual advances have been made, and you can leave with your head held high.

Just think how things might end if you take the direct approach and say what you mean, rather than speaking in code . . . the rejection won't be subtle, it will be a glass of wine thrown publicly in your face and you'll have to leave with your head held in a tea-towel.

The problem for most of us is that talking in subtle metaphors isn't easy. Most of us have familiar chat-up lines that we like to stick to, despite repeated failures over the years. Ever optimistic, we wheel these chat-up lines out and throw them at people we fancy in the hope of starting a flirtatious conversation. 'Get your coat, you've pulled', 'You don't sweat much for a fat lass', and 'How would you like your eggs in the morning?' may be clever, sophisticated lines★, but their directness ensures that the other person's curiosity is not engaged. Hitting them in this manner with overtly sexual advances can scare them off and

★That's meant to be ironic, by the way.

doesn't leave them wondering about you.

If there's nothing to wonder about you, there's no interest in you. So it's vital to talk to them in a mildly enigmatic way that makes them want to find out more. It's like a good crime novel: the reader is fed small clues throughout the book, but the murderer isn't revealed until the end. That makes the reader want to keep reading in order to find out that information. Keep details of yourself hidden for as long as possible (without saying so little that it looks like you have no conversation skills at all), and keep them guessing as to whether you really fancy them, what you're really like, and whether you're a murderer.

This drip-feeding of interesting information is when flirting really comes into its own. If it's going well, the other person will send test signals to you in their choice of conversation and body language. They want to see how you respond. This gives you the opportunity to flirt back with similar subtlety, and suddenly you're off. But give the game away in your opening line to them that you're desperate for a shag and there's nothing to play for, no flirting to be done. And the bottom line is that you're less likely to get that shag.

The most important rule of talking flirtatiously is to show interest in the other person. We all love to talk about ourselves, and we instinctively like people who encourage us to do so. If you give someone plenty of opportunities to blow their own trumpet, you're more likely to get to the point where they're blowing your trumpet. And if brass instrument euphemisms aren't your bag, just ask for a blow-job.

If you're stuck for things to ask them, just remember the basic questions: who, where, why, when, and how much for the night? Build your questions around these blocks in order to establish a firm rapport. From this rapport comes familiarity, which brings trust. This makes people more comfortable flirting.

It's also crucial to ask questions that invite more than a monosyllabic answer. There are many things you could ask someone that require just a *yes* or a *no* answer. 'Do you like this place?' for example is a dead-end question, answerable with *yes* or *no*. 'What is it that you like about this place?' is essentially the same question, but phrased in order to elicit a longer response: at the very least the reply will be *dunno*.

Don't fall into the trap of thinking that you are an interesting person and going to great lengths to explain why. You're not interesting: you're boring. You won't agree with that, because we all think we're the most fascinating person on the planet, but actually we're all boring to other people. And yet we all love nothing more than to talk about our lives, our beliefs and our ambitions to others. They may not appear bored by it, but underneath the polite façade they are yawning uncontrollably. This is why it's so crucial to get the person you want to flirt with to talk about themselves and to stifle your own yawns. Fake that keen interest in their life story, and don't interrupt too much with parallels from your own life. They don't want to hear about them.

It's useful to be the listener, the

interviewer, because by making them answer your questions you can build their trust and then begin the subtle process of steering those questions towards flirtatious subjects: their relationships; their attitudes to sex; even their most bizarre sexual experiences and favourite perversions.

Not recommended

Some 'traditional' flirting techniques are no longer appropriate and won't win you any favours. Wolf whistles and bum pinching seemed to work well in *Carry On* films, but in reality they only worked on Barbara Windsor and these days a writ for sexual harassment is a more likely result than a smile and an 'Ooh, cheeky!'. Saying 'Blimey!' when a pretty girl comes into the room is just sad. Commenting on an impressive chest with 'I bet you don't get many of those to the pound' will get you into all sorts of trouble: you have to measure them in kilos these days.

Physical contact

Humans have evolved a natural instinct towards bodily contact. Our ancestors could make love to anyone, anywhere, anytime, without self-consciousness or social repression. But the sixties are over now, and more subtle techniques apply these days.

Love-making is the ultimate form of physical contact, and that is what we usually aspire to when flirting with someone. For women there are hundreds of subtly different levels of contact that lead to the love-making stage; for men there is only the fumble with the bra catch and the fruitless search for the G-spot.

Learning the more subtle forms of physical contact is crucial when flirting. A gentle invasion of someone's personal space can result in mild contact at the arms, the legs, or even the breast. If this contact is accepted, you're all set to go further. If the other person attempts to re-establish their personal space, perhaps using military force or razor wire, make your excuses and leave.

Footsie

Footsie is one of the best-loved flirting techniques. It can be played under restaurant tables or office desks, and in a slightly more open way it can be played simply when sitting next to someone on a sofa or standing next to them. There's no need to go straight in with removing your shoe and sensually rubbing your toes up someone's leg. That's tantamount to coming out with a chat-up line like 'What winks and is great in bed?' and then winking at them. It's far safer to begin by aligning your foot with theirs and applying a little bit of pressure. It's the sort of thing that could happen by mistake very easily, so if their foot recoils from you all you need say is that you thought it was the chair leg or a bag. If the foot stays there, try increasing the pressure. It will either lead to one of you stroking the other one's foot, or to a battle for legroom under the table.

Setting up artificial reasons for body contact

Physical contact can be instigated on the grounds of some kind of game or analysis. These techniques are great for flirting and can accelerate the process from initial chat to physical confidence with each other.

Palm reading

The most common form of 'artificially induced' contact, this works well at parties or in clubs and bars. No knowledge is required, and no one will expect a serious analysis of skin lines. But it gives you the opportunity to take the other person's hand in your own and to run your fingers over their skin. With a little confidence, this can be done in a more sensual way than a professional palm reader would do, whilst being fun and giving you the chance to say that the lines indicate a passionate person, bursting with sexual energy. Flattering someone within the context of a fake palm reading will boost their self-esteem, and will also make them like you more.

Eyeball reading

Similar to above, but make sure your breath is fresh before attempting this one. Stand right up against their face, noses touching, and pretend to read the lines in their irises. Talk any old romantic crap about them, mentioning that their destiny lies with a type of person that is basically you. When the eyeball reading is over, you will have invaded their personal space in an intimate way, and if you've done a good job at flirting with them and entertaining them at the same time that barrier should remain down. If they step back from you afterwards and offer you a minty sweet, things haven't gone so well.

Buttock reading

Perfect for parties, a (bare) buttock reading gets you straight into someone's underwear without the need for all that complicated talking and subtle flirting. You can also squeeze and caress the buttocks as part of your analysis. There won't be many barriers to overcome once someone has dropped their pants for you and showed you their spotty arse. Put one palm against the centre of each buttock (assuming they have two of them) and feel their arse-energy trickle between your fingers. Talk them through the process in a calm, doctor-like way, to give them confidence in your ability to talk a load of new-age crap whilst groping them. Gently squeeze both halves together, then pat them in a downward motion from the top. Then run your fingers gently up from the top of the leg along the arse-crack, making up some kind of legitimate-sounding reason for doing so as you go along. Remember to wash your hands after you've finished.

Remember that if someone actually agrees to let you read

their buttocks, then the chances are that they either fancy you, or that they hate you but have an enormous fart brewing.

Massage

We all love a good massage. Learn some basic techniques of neck and back massage, and drop into the conversation that you love to give massages. If the other person then hints at back problems or a stiff neck, they are inviting you to offer a massage. If the subject rapidly changes to the weather or railways, put that massage oil back in your pocket.

Arm wrestling

Not the most romantic way to begin a relationship, but a useful ice-breaker if you don't have the confidence to offer a buttock reading. Don't be too competitive, though. You're not likely to get anywhere with someone if you break their arm within minutes of meeting them.

Body language

Just as the verbal language of flirting is conducted in code, interpreting a person's body language also means understanding a code. At its most basic level, we all know the difference between a smile and a frown. That's the kind of body language we encounter all the time. The language expressed by the face is easy to read because it's there in front of you. But it's equally important to understand the language of other parts of the body, and of the body as a whole.

Facial expressions

These are one of the easiest indicators of a person's emotions to read. Flirting is all about reading the other person's thoughts without those thoughts being overtly expressed: a blank face can make it difficult to judge how well your flirting attempts are going, but an emotive face will act as a scoreboard, lighting up the results of the match as you go. Smile when you're flirting and you should receive smiles back.

Eye contact

This is a relatively easy way to detect a person's interest in you, although you won't know about it unless you're capable of maintaining eye contact yourself. Successful flirting involves staring into someone's eyes for longer than would ordinarily feel comfortable.

Introverts naturally find this difficult, extroverts just do it and don't think about it. If the other person maintains eye contact whilst talking to you, it shows enthusiasm for your company. If they only glance at you occasionally then you can assume that they are either bored or shy.

Shyness will manifest itself in other forms, such as a lack of forthright opinions, a quiet voice and very little conversation. All these symptoms together mean that the person is finding it hard to talk to you because of their introverted nature, rather than because you're boring them. But if an apparently confident person won't keep eye contact with you, you've lost them. Move on.

A popular technique for establishing initial eye contact with a stranger is to catch their eye, then look down at the ground. If you have sparked any fascination in them at all, they will still be looking at you when you look up. If they've emigrated in the meantime, you've lost them again. Move on.

Winking

Those of you who excitedly read the title of this sub-chapter a little too quickly and are about to be disappointed that it covers ways of closing one eye whilst keeping the other open should refer to a sister title to this book, *Kama Sutra For One*, also published by

Summersdale. Winking is a cheesy and old-fashioned technique for flirting with someone. A wink can indicate a private connection between two people that makes them both feel more special than the others in the room. More typically, though, it simply means 'I'd like to shag you'. If carried out with panache and confidence it can be a fun ingredient in a flirtatious situation. If carried out badly, you'll look like you have a problem with a contact lens.

Arms

Some people are very tactile when chatting and will gesticulate, touch, and even cuddle you without any provocation. Oh, you haven't met this person yet? You've only experienced arms crossed tightly across the chest until you leave them alone? Yes, that's the other side of the body language of arms. It's a very simple code. Don't apply the tactile approach to someone with crossed arms. Aim instead to balance your movements and positions with theirs.

Legs

If you're chatting someone up and you suddenly notice their legs are running away from you very fast, it's usually a hint that your flirting attempts are not appreciated. More helpful signs are legs outstretched in a relaxed manner (if sitting down), or standing 'at ease' with feet apart.

Feet

There is a theory that if someone points their toes at you, it means they fancy you. This is not the most scientifically sound theory ever made, since it would mean shoe shop assistants and chiropodists would all think they were the most desirable people on the planet. Still, check out the other person's toes and see which way they point. If you think they might believe in that kind of crap themselves, point your toes at them just to get them excited.

If you're in an environment in which there's no music playing, a tapping toe indicates impatience. This could mean that you're talking too much about yourself and need to switch the attention back to the other person. If the latest dance hits are booming around you then the tapping toe could still mean impatience, however. The owner of the toe clearly would rather be dancing than talking to you. Ask them to dance and use it as a means of entering their personal space.

Personal space

In Western society we have a concept of our own 'personal space'. Other cultures manage without setting up this imaginary force field around themselves, but our restrained upbringings encourage a space of at least a couple of feet between us and any strangers. That's why we don't sit next to people on trains or buses unless we have to. It's why we leave a little gap between ourselves and the people next to us in a queue. The concept of personal space is vital in determining how well your flirting is going down. Learn to recognise the way in which other people maintain their personal space when you talk to them. It's usually enough space to avoid any physical contact, even when moving, and should keep you sufficiently far apart so you can't smell each other's breath. The process of flirting aims to break into that personal space, or rather to encourage the other person to invite you into it.

Dancing

The primitive mating ritual of dance goes all the way back to the days of disco. It's a means of simulating sexual moves, of demonstrating sexual suppleness and rhythm, and of proving that you're a hopeless dancer. Provided you can find the confidence to dance with some energy and enthusiasm, one-to-one dancing with a partner can be an excellent way of flirting without having to talk. Limited body contact is possible in most forms of dancing, but the best dance ever invented for flirts has to be the slow dance. This requires no more skill than the ability to hold on tightly to someone and shuffle your feet slowly whilst wondering whether or not to touch their bottom. It's probably a better idea to caress non-sexual parts of their body if you're not sure how they'll react (or if their boyfriend/girlfriend is watching). Run your hands up their spine, up their neck and into their hair, gently bringing their face towards you until you wake up.

Chat-up lines*

Why use a chat-up line?

The whole point of using a chat-up line is to break the ice with a stranger. Many chat-up lines sound corny or cheesy, or are downright rude, but that's because it's hard to start a conversation with someone you fancy without your intentions being obvious. If it's apparent that you're only talking to them on the off-chance of getting a shag, you

* For a full collection of chat-up lines, refer to a copy of *The Little Book of Chat-up Lines*, published by Summersdale.

might as well be up front about it and use a witty line. But it's better if you can be more subtle and approach someone for what appears to be a genuine reason, unconnected to your throbbing loins. These 'genuine' approaches are less likely to scare anyone off, although it may take you longer to steer the conversation towards sexual matters because you have initially gone off in the wrong direction. A direct chat-up line, on the other hand, will either give you a head start to where you want to go or will fail instantly (the latter being more common, sadly).

Top 10 most commonly used chat-up lines

1
Get your coat, you've pulled.

2
You can use my phone to call your mum and tell her you're not coming home tonight.

3
Do you come here often?

4
If I said you had a beautiful body would you hold it against me?

5
What's a girl like you doing in a place like this?

6

I didn't believe in love at
first sight until I saw you.

7

Is that a gun in your pocket or are
you just pleased to see me?

8

How would you like your
eggs in the morning?

9

Can I buy you a drink?

10

I suppose a shag's out
of the question?

Top 10 genuine-sounding chat-up lines

1
I'm sure I know
you from somewhere.

2
Have you got the time?

3
Do you have a light?

4
Excuse me, I'm looking
for the toilets.

5
Didn't you go to my school?

6
Can you give me a hand?

7
Can I help you with that?

8
Do you mind if I introduce myself?

9
Is this seat taken?

10
Hello.

Top 10 cheesy chat-up lines

1

People tell me I've got a one track mind: shall we pull into the sidings and couple?

2

Excuse me, I'm new around here. Can you give me directions to your bedroom?

3

The best thing about you would have to be my arms.

4

Congratulations! You've won first prize in a competition: a date with me!

5

I love you.

6

**Do you believe in love at first sight,
or should I walk past you again?**

7

**Who stole the stars out of the sky
and put them in your eyes?**

8

**Let me introduce myself:
I'm your future husband.**

9

How did you get to be so beautiful?

10

**'Yes' is my favourite word.
What's yours?**

Top 10 sexy chat-up lines

1
What winks and is great in bed?
(wink)

2
Nice legs. When do they open?

3
**I've got a condom with
your name on it.**

4
**I'll show you mine if you
show me yours.**

5
**I'd like to lick your belly-button . . .
from the inside.**

6
**You make me feel like a squirrel. I'd
like to pile my nuts up against you.**

7
How about I sit on your lap and
we'll see what pops up?

8
Do you fancy going halves
on a bastard?

9
Let's go skinny-dipping together.

10
I feel like I already know you
because I've undressed you
completely in my mind.

Top 10 witty chat-up lines

1
Hi, I'm a postman, so you can rely on me to deliver a large package.

2
Hi, I'm a meteorologist, and I've been admiring your warm front.

3
Hi, I'm here on a computer date, but the computer hasn't shown up.

4
Hi, I'm a doctor: what's your appendix doing tonight? I'd love to take it out.

5
I can read you like a book. I bet you're great between the covers.

6
I'm like quick-drying cement: after I've been laid it doesn't take me long to get hard.

7

Let's get something straight
between us.

8

Hi, I'm from Wonderbra. We're
conducting free spot checks to make
sure our customers are wearing the
correct size bras. Just breathe out
slowly once my hands are in place.

9

Have you got any Irish in you? Would
you like some?

10

Are your legs tired? You've been
running through my mind all day.

Flirting on the Internet, e-mail and texting

Face-to-face flirting requires more courage than long distance communications, so many people find it easier to open their hearts and expose their emotions and desires using the written word. What was once the preserve of love letters has become that of e-mails, text messages and Internet chat rooms. Chat rooms permit real-time written word dialogues with people in any part of the world. It's easy to flirt confidently with someone who can't see your face or hear your voice, and who probably never will. This makes the Internet an excellent medium for developing skills and experience of flirting.

There are websites that are designed for flirting. They will send e-mail messages anonymously on your behalf, sometimes with an animated greetings card.

Whenever you get hold of someone's mobile phone number, send them a nice, flirty text message. It's definitely the way of the future.

Premium rate telephone services

These services are unparalleled as a means of practising your chat-up technique with faceless strangers (except by getting a job as a randy nurse in a facial burns unit), but if you really want to flirt via telephone then be ready to pay the price. Using the sort of dating or flirting telephone lines advertised on television and in magazines will help you to develop confidence, conversational skills and infeasibly high telephone bills. Remember you can save a lot of money simply by not dialling any numbers and flirting into the telephone regardless. Or call a freephone help line if you need to spend hours talking down the line to someone you don't know and just flirt with whoever answers the call. They're probably bored senseless by their job anyway. And if you absolutely must use the premium rate flirting services, please make sure you're not the person responsible for paying the bill (I never said this book was about morals).

Dating agencies

Whether through Internet introductions or real meetings, dating agencies offer a legitimate and fun way of getting to meet and flirt with other single people. It's usually an expensive process, but if you're starting again after a long relationship or a divorce and none of your friends are single it's a better way of meeting potential partners than by hanging out in bars on your own looking desperate. If you end up on a date with someone who doesn't float your boat, use it as a practice session that will give you greater confidence for the next time.

For safety reasons always arrange to meet someone met via the Internet in a public place, and for lunch rather than for an evening meal. Never reveal your surname, home address or telephone number until you have met them and are sure you like them, unless you've always fancied the idea of having a stalker.

Alcohol

Flirting whilst drunk is both good and bad. It's good because it relaxes the body's muscles, including the brain, and a relaxed brain is less fearful. The less fear you feel the more confident you seem, and therefore the more attractive you become. The downside is that for many of us there is a fine line between drinking enough alcohol to create that confidence (or Dutch courage) and drinking a little too much so that you start to act like a bit of a twat. Once you become over-confident, slurring your words and swaying on your feet, the attractiveness diminishes to the point where you would have been better off staying sober and nervous.

Drinks, even non-alcoholic ones, are also a useful prop to hide nerves. If you feel self-conscious in a social situation it can be hard to know what to do with your hands, and holding a cigarette or a glass has long played a useful role in that respect.

Taking it to the edge

The limits of flirting are different for everyone. Most of us feel uncomfortable just trying to maintain a pleasant conversation with a stranger and would not consider being too directly sexual or weird. Yet there are those whose flirting technique involves asking a stranger for a shag, or taking their clothes off unexpectedly, or putting on an act of pretending that they have been having a relationship with the stranger for years and seeing if the stranger plays along with it. There's no point in trying extreme methods to impress someone if you're not prepared to handle the extreme varieties of rejection that will almost certainly follow (and which might involve prosecution if you take things too far in the wrong context).

As an example, the technique of approaching strangers and asking for a shag without so much as a word of introduction or even asking their names will generate many kinds of unpleasant rejections, but one or two times in a hundred it will generate a success. If you have the mental (and possibly physical) strength to handle a 98 per cent rejection rate then good luck to you. But if you want to minimise the possibility and severity of rejections then play it safe and subtle.

How far can you go with a stranger?

By definition, not very far. As soon as you get intimate with a stranger, they cease to be a stranger. Daft question, when you think about it. Unless you're snogging someone you haven't been formally introduced to, in which case technically you are still strangers.

When does flirting become cheating?

Flirting makes us feel alive. It gives us confidence and it's fun to play the game of laying the foundations of a potential sexual relationship even if you don't intend actually to get physical with the other person. So if you're already in a relationship and you get flirting with someone you meet at a party, how far can you take it without actually being unfaithful? This kind of depends on your perspective. If your intention is to flirt verbally but not physically and for it not to go beyond mere saucy words, then few people would consider it to be unfaithful. If your intentions were more dishonourable, however, then any level of flirting, whether successful or not, could be considered unfaithful. On the other hand, if you don't get anywhere then who's to know whether you intended cheating or not? In the end it's going to come down to an individual's (or a couple's) definition of what constitutes infidelity. This can range from verbal flirtation, through minor body contact, all the way to full sexual intercourse. Some don't even consider the latter to be a problem provided it happens only once. If you're in a relationship and would like to flirt with others, it's a good idea to agree on acceptable boundaries with your partner so that your conscience can remain clear.

The worst that can happen

Try to put into perspective all the fears and worries that hold you back from flirting with someone. After all, what's the worst that can happen? Embarrassment, rejection, humiliation, physical violence, depression, and an overdose. OK, things can get pretty rough out there, but we all get knocked back occasionally and if you never try anything you'll never get anywhere. Making an initial approach to a stranger rarely results in anything worse than a polite rejection. So what? That's not going to stop you trying, is it? They don't know your name and they'll never see you again, so why let it worry you?

Making someone
want to flirt with you

It's much easier to flirt with someone if they want to flirt with you. But how can this apparent miracle be achieved? What is it about some lucky people that make them attractive to others, whilst more unfortunate people only manage to repulse those whom they would like to shag? We always assume it's down to the way someone looks, which gives an unfair and unearned advantage to good-looking people. But looks are only half of the package of ingredients that determines someone's attractiveness. The rest of the ingredients are inside the person. They consist of a person's characteristics, their outlook on life, their sense of humour, their confidence, their affability, their social skills, and their sense of self-worth. All these things together are potentially capable of overcoming any physical shortcomings. Let's look at them in detail.

Your internal characteristics

Outlook on life

How do you perceive your general temperament? Try to see yourself as someone else might see you. If you were in their shoes, would you want to befriend yourself, or would you frighten yourself away? Do you have an approach to life that is positive and which makes people warm to you, or are you mostly negative, cynical, complaining and uncharitable? Look at other people whose personalities you find attractive. What seems to be their outlook on life? They probably don't seem to take themselves seriously. They probably appear laid-back and carefree. Would you be more appealing if you emulated their approach?

Sense of humour

Most people rank a good sense of humour amongst the most attractive facets of a potential lover. It's not necessary to be a stand-up comedian to qualify in this respect, merely to have the ability to laugh generously and also to laugh at yourself. If the other person makes a joke, be sure to laugh. We all find different types of humour funny, and it's easy to feel an intellectual connection to someone who laughs at the same jokes that we do.

Confidence

Of all the internal and external characteristics that make up an individual, confidence is the most important when it comes to flirting. It's virtually true to say that confidence equals attractiveness.

This is problematic because very few people actually feel confident outside of their home environment. Fear is a real factor that limits the things we do and the things we say: fear of embarrassment, ridicule, punishment or humiliation, and even fear of simply sticking our heads above the parapet and getting noticed. It is this fear that makes most people dress conservatively (and makes them dress at all). Fear stops us saying what we are really thinking and from doing what we would prefer to be doing. In the context of flirting, fear causes a number of problems which can only be overcome with confidence.

1. Fear of making an initial approach to someone.
2. Fear of letting someone know that you fancy them.
3. Fear of asking too many questions about them in case you appear nosy.
4. Fear that they won't fancy you.
5. Fear that you're boring them.
6. Fear of rejection.
7. Fear that your wife or husband will catch you out.

Most people would look at that list of fears and identify one or

more (if not all) that apply to
them. And yet the human race
breeds on thanks primarily to our
ability to drum up sufficient
confidence to overcome these
fears and get flirting (and because
the Revd. Thomas Malthus'
predictions of a population
explosion followed by mass
starvation have yet to come true).
But all this still fails to address the
issue of how confident you feel
inside, and the chances are that
you don't think you're as
confident as most other people.
Whenever you feel like that, just
be aware of one thing: no one is

truly confident. Remember that and it will give you confidence!

What about people who look completely at ease, unafraid of anything? (Don't you just hate them?) Well, they're not what they appear. They are people who have learned to generate an aura of confidence because they have become accustomed to dealing with particular sets of circumstances. Think of your first day at work: you were nervous, awkward, embarrassed at taking your clothes off in front of all those strangers. Oh, I was assuming you work as a life model or a stripper, by the way. It helps me when I'm thinking through these examples. Anyway, the next time you did it, the fear diminished slightly. After several weeks the job contained few surprises and you were able to cope with it. Deep inside you couldn't really believe you were actually doing it and it scared you, but on the surface you had achieved a veneer of confidence.

Take another, less draughty, example. Suppose you were employed to chat to people in a bar, one after the other, to demonstrate spoons to them.

The first time you approach a stranger it's going to be very tough for you. The second time is a little easier, and after a while it's a doddle. The confidence grows with familiarity, and this can be applied to any of the aspects of flirting that scare you. By putting yourself in the situation that frightens you time and again, you will build a resistance to the fear and will start to appear confident.

That's fair enough for the long term, but how do you tackle an imminent flirting session that means everything to you and yet scares the pants off you? The only quick fix is to fake confidence. Try pretending you're someone else. Imagine you're much more wealthy, much more experienced in life, more travelled and more cultured. Try imagining that you're famous and that when you walk into a room heads turn and people start whispering that you're the person they hate off the telly, and yet they all want to be your friend in case you can get them into the Groucho Club. Convince yourself that you're better than anyone else present, and you'll find that you have become confident in their presence. You can't give your flirting a better start than to enter a room filled with what I call fake confidence, or, to give it its more common name, alcohol.

Affability

Self-important pomposity won't win you many friends. Being friendly and gentle can help the other person tackle their own fear of flirting with you. Make it easy for them by not scaring them off with a fierce persona and scowling expression. Just radiate warmth and love (but not too

much because hippies scare
people off, too).

Social skills

You're going to have to flirt in
various social situations for which
different social skills will apply (in
addition to your flirting skills – I
know, it's getting tough, but hang
in there). Your style of approach
needs to be appropriate to the
surroundings, and that's where
those social skills come in. These
skills are best learnt by watching
others. Look at how they hold a
glass, or a fork, or a cigarette.
Look at how they conduct

conversations, how they stand, how loudly they laugh. Fit in with people and people will want you.

Self-worth

If you don't value yourself highly, how can you expect anyone else to value you? Tell yourself that you are special. You are unique. You have a vital contribution to make to society. The world has been enriched by your presence. It's all nonsense, of course, but successful self-delusion has the same positive benefit as a sense of self-worth. Chant mantras to yourself every morning such as

'I am beautiful', 'I love myself and other people love me', and 'I am a success'. I know it's nauseating and might give you the same symptoms as morning sickness, but it's an essential part of the brainwashing process that will train you to think positively and create a sense of worth that will become apparent to others.

The alternative to this is to be perceived as needy and weak, as someone who will drain the energy from a relationship rather than contributing to it. Although you might be lucky enough to find someone who enjoys helping needy people to love themselves, the chances are your partner will find it a chore that saps their emotions.

Your external characteristics

Style

You've either got it or you haven't got it. Or you've got it to some extent. That probably covers most eventualities. But how do you know if you've got it or not, and what does it actually mean? After all, everyone has *a* style, even if it's a pissy, smelly and obnoxious style that repels everyone. Your style is the way you dress, the way you do your hair, the shoes you wear, the make-up or facial hair you have.

Most people adopt a generic style that enables them to blend in with the culture in which they live. In Western societies, for instance, this means that men usually wear shoes. But there are many types of shoes, each of which can depict a different style. Sandals say something about you, as do rubber boots, leather brogues and trainers. People make assumptions about your personality, social class and attitudes on the basis of the style you present to them. Of course this is unfair and morally wrong, but we all do it. You'll make very different assumptions about someone in a smart suit and someone in ripped jeans and a T-shirt.

Think about the way in which you present yourself and what that will make others think about you. Are you giving out a message that you're well balanced, safe and nice? Or do you look as if you don't wash, have no friends and murder hitch-hikers for a hobby? Subconsciously we're all concerned when we meet someone that they might be a dangerous freak. That's why we're more comfortable with strangers when they are introduced to us via a mutual friend. Complete strangers are all potential murderers. It may sound extreme, but that attitude is a defensive instinct that has evolved over thousands of generations. However, we are less afraid of people who dress similarly to us. They give us confidence that they are from the same culture and that they believe in the same things as us.

So when thinking about your style, look at the styles of others around you. Try to stick to current fashions that will make other people comfortable in your presence. Individuality is great, but only if you can create that individuality within the confines of a known style, otherwise you will simply appear to be a freak. Remember to adapt and change your outward style as fashions change over the years. Many people make the mistake of finding a fashion they like and sticking with it for the rest of their lives, while others around them move on. Eventually they begin to look a bit sad, and their social acceptability wanes. It has nothing to do with what you feel makes you look good: you have to be cynical and objective if you want to adopt a style that will enhance your flirting chances.

Smells

Don't ignore any of the senses when flirting. What you look like and what you say are obviously important, but the other person will probably have a nose and will not want to smell you unless you have a pleasant fragrance. No one is going to flirt with you if you forgot to shower today (or this week). Bath or shower daily, use a good deodorant, and spray on a reasonable amount of perfume or aftershave. But don't over do it: too much perfume will make heads turn for the wrong reasons.

Hair

People are shallow. We make assumptions all day, every day, about other people, and this is always based on the way they look. So how you cut, style, colour and present your hair will affect the way you are perceived by others. If you get it right for the section of society within which you wish to flirt, they might not think anything about you, but get it wrong and they will start to think negatively about your class, education, political stance, occupation, sexuality and personality. The safest bet for easy flirting is to blend in with those around you. Standing out from the crowd demands much more strength of personality and that makes successful flirting harder.

Body shape

It's rare to find someone who is truly happy with their body shape. The chances are that your negative perception of your own body is a source of self-consciousness which can only hinder your flirting technique. There are several things you can do about this:

1. Work on your body. To get to your preferred shape, try a sensible diet, work out in the gym, sacrifice a few cakes in the noble cause of flirting. (How's that for glib, oversimplified advice? There's no room in this little book for a full account of the mental struggles involved in losing weight, and how we often eat pies because we're unhappy, then we're unhappy because we're fat, so we eat even more pies. You'll

have to deal with that conundrum on your own.)

2.   Dress in sympathy with your body shape, i.e. hide the flab.

3.   Target someone who seems to have a similar or worse body shape than you do, so that you don't feel at a disadvantage.

Make-up

A thick layer of foundation, some strong eyeshadow and bright lipstick can create a mask behind which you can flirt with increased confidence. Works for the ladies, too.

Getting rid of a persistent flirt

It's hard to get rid of someone without being rude. You know the rejection is going to hurt them, and sometimes it's better to lie in order to spare their feelings. If someone you don't fancy is coming on strong to you then telling them you're married or that you have a prior date or appointment lets them down without it being a reflection on them. But if you come out and tell them to piss off because they're ugly, that might tend to hurt them.

Put downs

Part of your flirting skills is the need to be able to get rid of someone politely and without causing them offence. If you're stuck with a person who is flirting with you when you would rather be flirting with someone else in the room, you might miss the chance to introduce yourself to the love of your life if you can't extricate yourself.

Put downs can convey different meanings, so here are a few classic examples.

Subtle put downs

I just need to visit the loo. I'll catch up with you later.

I have to go now, but I'd love to meet up again some time. [liar!] Here's my card.

I've just remembered I was meant to call someone. I'll be back in a minute.

Direct but sensitive put downs

I think I ought to tell you that I'm already with someone.

It's been great meeting you, but I have to dash to an appointment.

There's someone else I promised to speak to tonight. If I don't catch up with you again have a good evening.

Direct and shitty put downs

Sorry, you're not my type.

Are you chatting me up? Stop it!

If you were the last person on earth I'd still rather sleep with my dog.

Stalking

Overenthusiastic, sustained flirting attempts aimed at one person can easily cross the line to become stalking. Be aware of their responses and willingness to indulge in flirting with you. If they want it to stop, you had better stop immediately otherwise court action and public humiliation will follow, not to mention the distress you will cause them. If you feel you are developing an obsession with someone who hasn't shown any interest in you, force yourself to try flirting with others. Don't lose your sense of perspective or self-respect. No one will be attracted to someone with an obsession.

Flirting in competition
(out-flirting someone else)

If you and someone else are going for the same person, remember this: the person you're both trying to attract will feel the same insecurities as you. They will fear rejection, fear making a fool of themselves if they think they are being chatted-up and flirt back only to find they were mistaken. So they want to be sure that they are doing the right thing in flirting with you, and if your rival makes them feel more confident about flirting than you do, your rival will win the prize. In other words, make sure your target knows you are serious about your flirting, because they won't want to take a chance with you if they know someone else really is serious about them. This goes against the rules of subtlety, but in these circumstances you simply need to progress more quickly from the subtle, metaphorical chat-up techniques to the directly romantic topics of conversation.

If the presence of a rival makes you nervous, you will be less attractive. Try to forget about your rival, and try not to care too much. The suitor who doesn't try too hard will be the most attractive, but if you give the other person too much space they will squeeze you out. It's all about finding a difficult balance between feigned indifference and displaying your interest.

On the rebound

People always seem to advise caution when trying to flirt with someone new immediately after a relationship has ended. The assumption is that it takes time for the emotions to settle, and until then any judgement will be clouded by the dregs of the old affair. But the caution should only apply to long-term decisions: in the short term you should just go for it. Flirting like crazy in order to boost your ego after rejection is highly recommended, and don't let recent rejection hold you back from taking chances. If there are lessons to be learned from the failed relationship then try to implement them at the start of the next one.

How do you know if someone is flirting with you?

This should be fairly obvious, but you want to be careful not to misinterpret someone who is simply being friendly. Usually a flirt will show good eye contact, a clear interest in you, and will smile at you. Then again, so will a friendly person. Perhaps the flirt doesn't seem so friendly with other people in the room? Perhaps you sense the conversation is being steered by them towards romantic topics? Perhaps they've asked you to drop your pants so that they can read your buttocks? There are many potential signs of flirting, and if you suspect someone is chatting you up and you want to respond positively, then try some of the techniques in this book and monitor the reaction. If they didn't intend to be flirtatious and they realise you are now flirting, the change in their tone should be clear. If they stay flirty after you've flirted back, then enjoy the rest of the evening. You won't need this book any more.

Develop your own flirting style

There's a lot to remember in this little book, and not every suggestion will be relevant to every person. That's why it's good to develop your own style of flirting. Use the techniques that you feel most comfortable with, and become confident in them. Your flirting style will then become part of your character, part of the charisma you radiate that attracts people to you. Always be ready to flirt, and that means always presenting yourself in the manner in which you feel most confident. Take the time to be clean, fresh and to wear your favourite clothes even if you're not planning on flirting that day: the best flirting experiences are the unexpected ones, and it would be awful to feel you can't indulge because you've forgotten to brush (or bring) your teeth today.

Top 10 do's and don'ts for flirting

Do

1. Smile.
2. Maintain eye contact.
3. Use the person's name.
4. Be generous in your praise for their clothes, hair, opinions etc.
5. Encourage them to tell you about themselves.
6. Relax in their company; regard them as old friends.
7. Find mutual connections in the people you know or the lives you lead.
8. Gently tease the conversation towards romance without being direct.
9. Read their body language.
10. Be attractive to yourself so that you become attractive to others.

Don't

1. Let rejection get you down. Learn from it and move on.
2. Give too much away about yourself immediately. Learn the attractiveness of being enigmatic.
3. Cling or appear needy.
4. Fidget or look awkward.
5. Wait for things to happen. Make them happen.
6. Think about how well you're doing. Just be natural.
7. Forget to be a good listener.
8. Drink too much.
9. Aim too high – go for people you think will be attracted to you.
10. Worry if none of this works the first time. Keep trying: it will work eventually.

The personality test

Pretend to be conducting a survey as part of a course or for a magazine article. Type out a list of questions which answer everything you'd like to know about a potential lover. An example list would be:

Name: Age:
Marital status: Occupation:
Favourite music: Hobbies:
Favourite food: Politics:
Preferred holiday destination:
Most interesting sexual experience:
Ideal lover:

Add your own questions to the list so that the answers give you enough information about someone to decide whether you still want to try flirting with them. Not only does the false questionnaire break the ice, giving you a legitimate and non-sexual reason for talking to them, but it gives you conversational topics and enables you to avoid those embarrassing faux pas when you state your strong dislike of something only to find that the other person loves it.

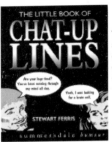

The Little Book of Chat-up Lines
The pocket collection of all the most hilarious chat-up lines and devastating put downs ever uttered.

How to Chat-up Babes
Full of tips to boost your confidence with the opposite sex, no single bloke should enter a bar without this package tucked in his trousers.

Je t'aime
How to say 'I Love You' in 100 languages

Learn how to say 'I Love you' in 100 different languages from Gaelic to Greek, from Eskimo to Esperanto and from Latin to Latvian.

The Little Book of Essential English Swear Words

Thicker, wider, longer lasting - yes, you too can have a vocabulary that impresses your friends, family and prospective employers.

BY THE SAME AUTHOR:

Love
*99 Ways to Show
You Care*

An amusing and enter-
taining collection of
inventive, imaginative,
and insane ways to say
the three most roman-
tic words in the English
language... 'I Love you'.